# H.O.U.S.E.*

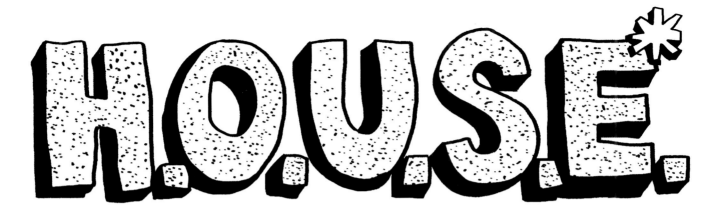

# H.O.U.S.E.

**H**OMES THAT ARE
**O**UTRAGEOUS,
**U**NBELIEVABLE,
**S**PECTACULAR AND
**E**XTRAORDINARY

ALEKSANDRA MIZIELIŃSKA ⌂ DANIEL MIZIELIŃSKI
TRANSLATED BY ELŻBIETA WÓJCIK-LEESE

HARPER
DESIGN
*An Imprint of HarperCollins Publishers*

The world is **full of houses**: big ones and small ones, high ones and low ones, pretty ones and ugly ones. We see them every day, and in some of them we spend a great deal of our lives. In fact, we are so used to houses that we barely notice them anymore, nor do we ask ourselves **where** they come from and **why** they look the way they do.

This book was made to change all that, and to show you that a house can be something extraordinary and **fascinating** because incredible, **jaw-dropping** houses really exist — not only in fairy tales and movies! You will learn from this book that a house doesn't need to look the way we take for granted it

should. It doesn't need to have things like permanently separated rooms or walls, or even stand on the ground. It can be constructed from **bizarre materials** and shaped in **extraordinary** ways.

If you're up to the challenge, perhaps one day, thanks to you, there will be stunning and **remarkable buildings** around us, and our world will be more interesting. **And why is this so important?** Well, because where we live and how we live shape who we are. With a little imagination and a willingness to step outside the box, we can design a world where anything is possible!

**H.O.U.S.E.** is a splendid selection of **thirty-five houses from around the world.** They have been hand-picked by a think-tank of independent scientists. Their decision is one hundred per cent subjective and cannot be overruled.

EXAMPLE OF
HOUSE LOCATION

POLAND

THINK-TANK
OF INDEPENDENT
SCIENTISTS

# bubble
## house

ORIGINAL NAME

← IDEAL NAME

Discover fascinating details about your selected house. Find its **location.** Meet the **architects** who have designed and constructed it. Think of its **ideal name.**

(You can compare it with the original name, always in the top right corner.)

ARCHITECTS

Thanks to our specially-designed **icons,** you can discover whether a house has been built in a city or the middle of a forest. Find out whether it is environmentally friendly, made of wood, bricks, glass, steel, sand or possibly plastic. See if it is equipped with a kitchen or a study. Or maybe it is so small that it contains nothing more than a bedroom!

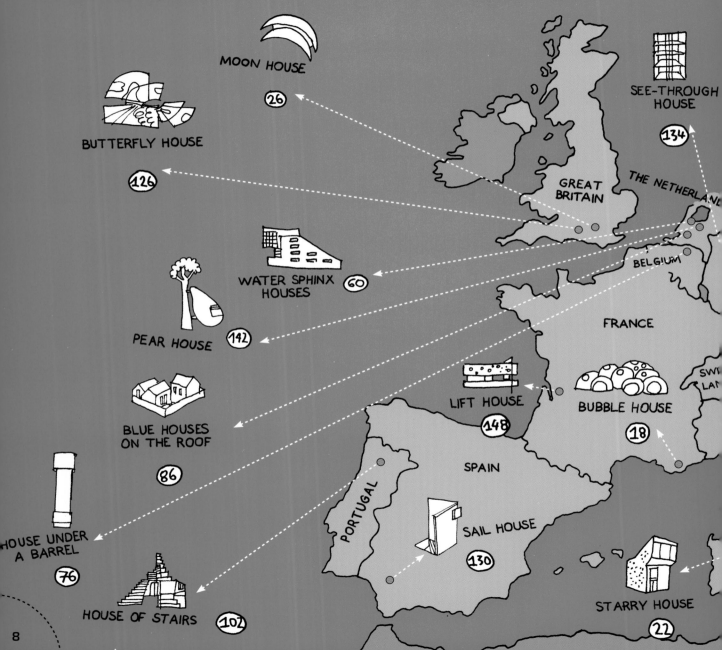

# HOUSES IN EUROPE

MOON HOUSE
26

BUTTERFLY HOUSE
126

WATER SPHINX HOUSES
60

PEAR HOUSE
142

BLUE HOUSES ON THE ROOF
86

HOUSE UNDER A BARREL
76

HOUSE OF STAIRS
102

SEE-THROUGH HOUSE
134

GREAT BRITAIN

THE NETHERLAND

BELGIUM

FRANCE

SWI
LAN

LIFT HOUSE
148

BUBBLE HOUSE
18

SPAIN

PORTUGAL

SAIL HOUSE
130

STARRY HOUSE
22

8

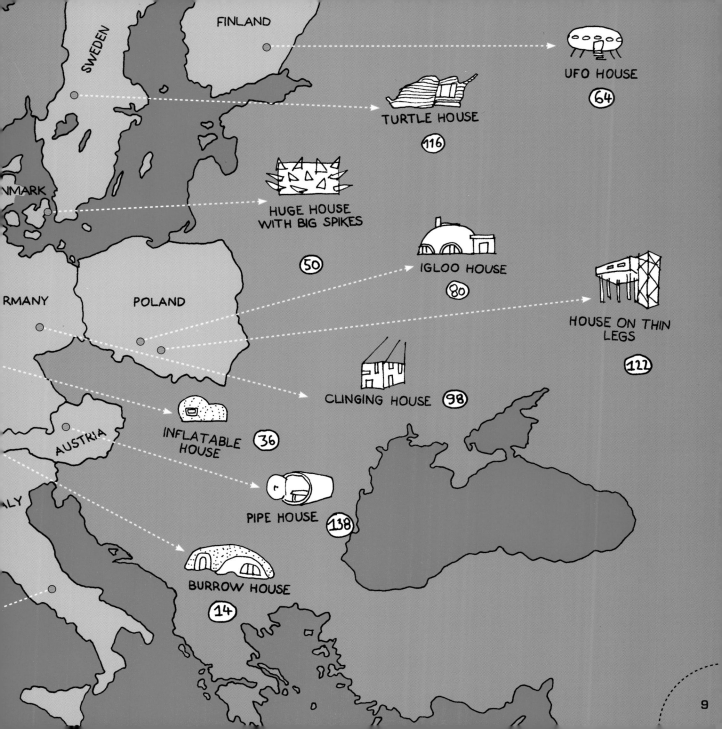

UFO HOUSE
**64**

TURTLE HOUSE
**116**

HUGE HOUSE
WITH BIG SPIKES
**50**

IGLOO HOUSE
**80**

HOUSE ON THIN
LEGS
**122**

CLINGING HOUSE **98**

INFLATABLE
HOUSE **36**

PIPE HOUSE **138**

BURROW HOUSE
**14**

FINLAND

SWEDEN

NMARK

RMANY

POLAND

AUSTRIA

ALY

9

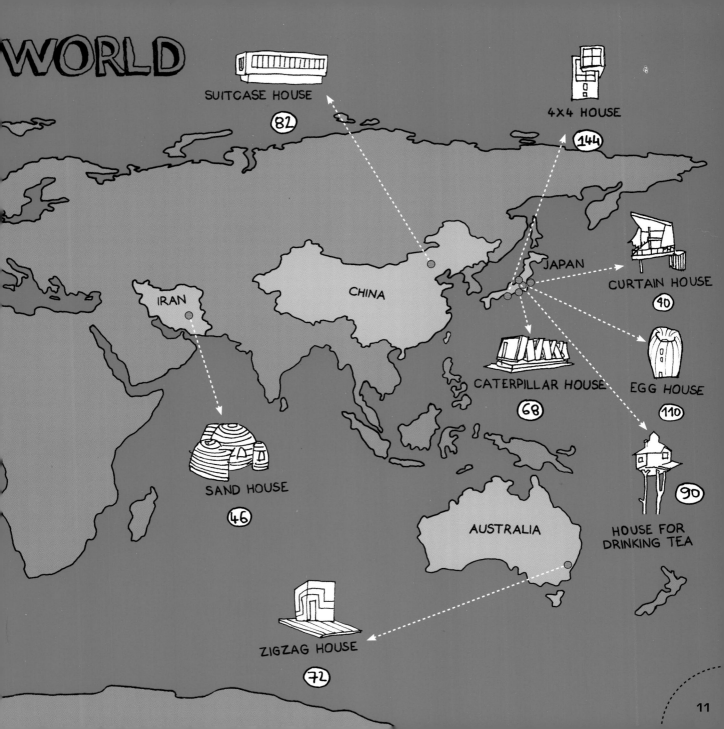

WORLD

SUITCASE HOUSE
82

4X4 HOUSE
144

CURTAIN HOUSE
40

JAPAN

IRAN

CHINA

CATERPILLAR HOUSE
68

EGG HOUSE
110

SAND HOUSE
46

HOUSE FOR
DRINKING TEA
90

AUSTRALIA

ZIGZAG HOUSE
72

# KEY

DATE THE HOUSE
WAS BUILT

HOUSE MADE OF
TIMBER

HOUSE MADE OF
CONCRETE

HOUSE MADE OF
GLASS

HOUSE MADE OF
BRICKS

HOUSE MADE OF
PLASTIC

PLASTIC IS A MAN-MADE MATERIAL.
IT CAN'T BE FOUND IN NATURE,
UNLIKE WOOD OR STONE.

HOUSE MADE OF
STEEL

HOUSE MADE OF
FABRIC

HOUSE MADE OF
SAND

A LITTLE HOUSE
FOR DRINKING TEA

THIS HOUSE HAS
A SLEEPING AREA

THIS HOUSE HAS
A BATHROOM

THIS HOUSE HAS
A KITCHEN

THIS HOUSE HAS
A STUDY

HOUSE MADE OF
SUSTAINABLE
MATERIALS

THIS MEANS THE HOUSE HAS BEEN MADE OUT OF MATERIALS WHICH CAN BE PRODUCED BY NATURE INDEFINITELY. TAKE, FOR EXAMPLE, TIMBER: IF WE PLANT MORE TREES THAN WE CUT DOWN, WE WILL ALWAYS HAVE SOME SPARE. BUT OIL AND COAL ARE NOT SUSTAINABLE, BECAUSE IT TAKES CENTURIES FOR THEM TO RENEW.

HOUSE USING
SOLAR ENERGY

HOUSE WITH
A RAINWATER TANK

HOUSE IN A
BIG CITY

HOUSE IN A
SMALL TOWN

HOUSE IN THE
COUNTRYSIDE
OR WILDERNESS

HOUSE IN THE
MOUNTAINS

HOUSE IN THE
FOREST

HOUSE BY
THE SEA

# burrow
## house

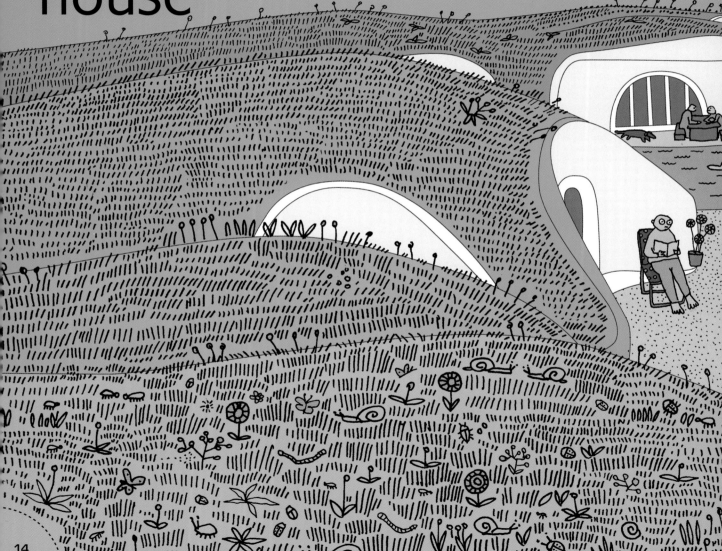

DIETIKON

SWITZERLAND

PETER VETSCH →

1993

15

Who on earth would like to **live in a burrow?** Nobody, surely. But come to think of it, burrows are in great demand among such creatures as the sly fox, timid rabbit or sneaky rat. Not to mention the fact that a comfortable hole in the ground—not too wet and not too dry, with something to sit on—is highly popular with hobbits.

Fascinated by the living habits of such hole-dwellers, Peter Vetsch designed a **fantasy settlement.** Nine houses surround a small artificial lake and create a tiny village. These curvy buildings are **covered with a thick layer of earth**—perfect for cultivating a garden or summer terrace, or arranging a playground.

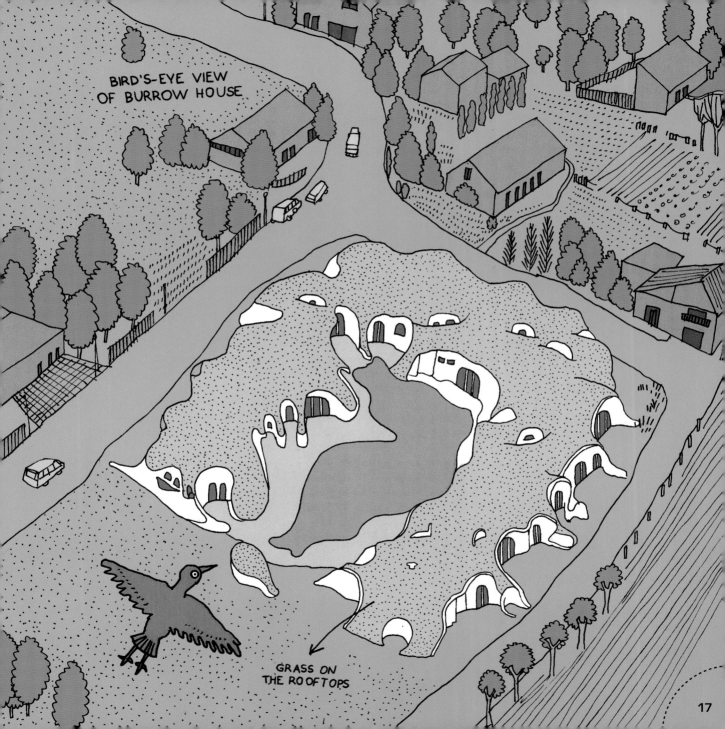

BIRD'S-EYE VIEW
OF BURROW HOUSE

GRASS ON
THE ROOFTOPS

# bubble
## house

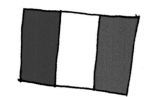

FRANCE

CÔTE D'AZUR
(FRENCH RIVIERA)

Think: bubbles. **Soap bubbles** shimmering with rainbows. The **air bubbles** you breathe out underwater in the bathtub or the swimming pool. Bubbles bubbling in a glass of juice as you blow through the straw. Bubbles rising to the surface as you pour yourself a fizzy drink.

All these **bubble beauties** are so enchanting that Antti Lovag has built several bubble houses. Bubbles, big and small; balls, baubles and spheres—all preserved in concrete and painted red.

ANTTI LOVAG

18

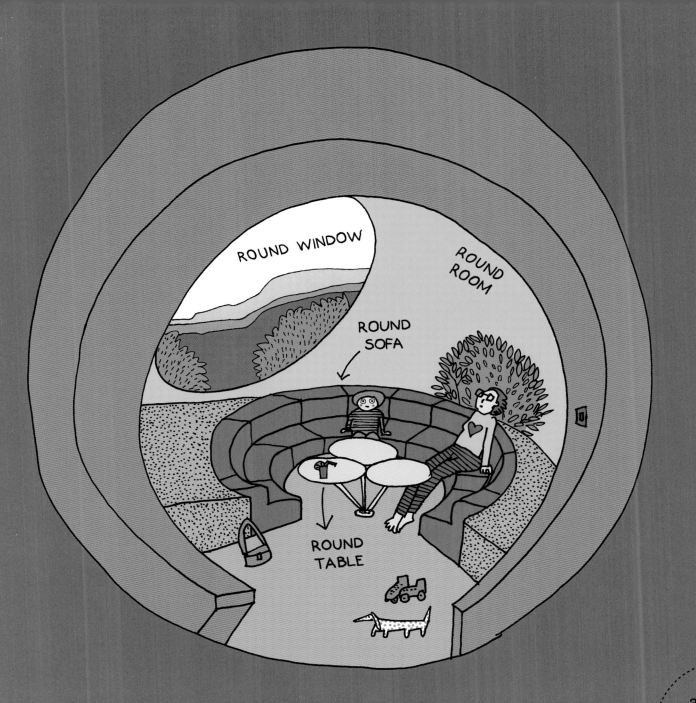

# starry
## house

LUCA GALOFARO

CARMELO
BAGLIVO

ITALY

ROME

STEFANIA MANNA

In the suburbs of Rome, Italy's capital city, there is a modest-looking orange house designed by the architects from the IaN+ studio. Nobody lives here, because inside there are **hydrobiology laboratories** and a huge room for important meetings.

Go to page 24 to see what happens in these labs.

In the Starry House, scientists from the University of Rome Tor Vergata examine everything to do with water, and often work late. At night, **small holes in one wall** twinkle like stars.

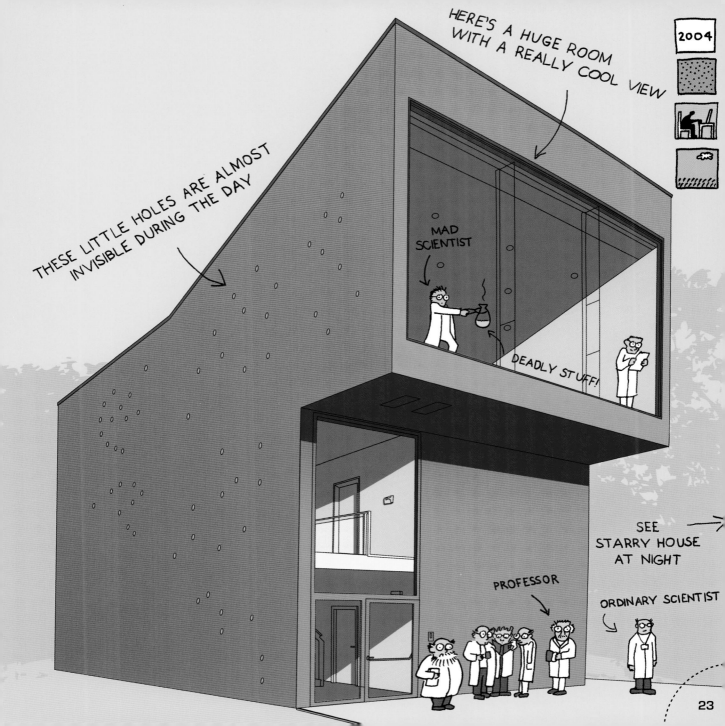

# WHAT HAPPENS IN HYDROBIOLOGY LABORATORIES

HERE WE INVESTIGATE EVERYTHING CONNECTED WITH WATER — WE CAN'T LIVE WITHOUT IT!

WATER

FISH

WATER SNAKE

FUNKY DIAGRAMS

MORE WATER

FILTHY WATER

CLEAN WATER

WATER FILTER

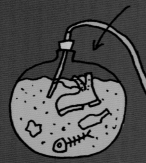

24

NOW THESE LITTLE HOLES LOOK LIKE STARS

PROFESSOR X

SLEEPY SCIENTISTS

SCIENTISTS ARE SO HARD-WORKING THAT THEY SOMETIMES SLEEP IN THEIR LABS

# moon
## house

WILTSHIRE

GREAT BRITAIN

The Moon isn't made of cheese, right? But Wallace and Gromit travelled all the way to the Moon for their cheese-tasting. On their arrival they were unpleasantly surprised by the Moon resident—a mechanical cheese caretaker. Ever wondered where he lived exactly?

**Instead of living on the Moon and orbiting the earth,** Ken Shuttleworth decided to live in a moon on Earth. But he didn't want to live in a full moon. So he used two quarters—or **two crescents**—to build half a moon, or a **whole house.**

The wall facing the garden is made of clear glass, so the residents have a beautiful view (with no cheese in sight). The other wall is not see-through, so they can enjoy some privacy.

KEN
SHUTTLEWORTH

1997

27

THE INTERIOR DECORATION CHANGES WITH THE SEASONS

RED FOR WINTER

YELLOW FOR SPRING

BLUE FOR SUMMER

BLACK AND WHITE IN THE AUTUMN

ENTRANCE →

KITCHEN

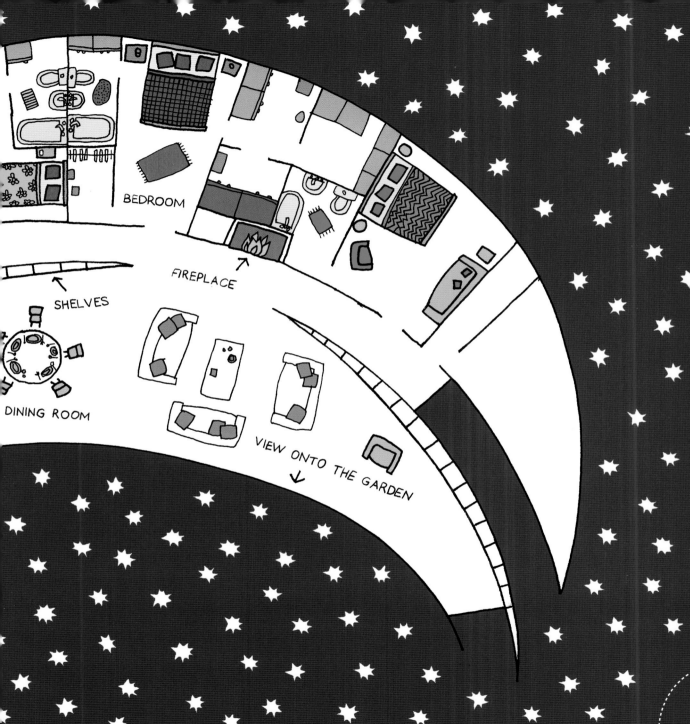

BEDROOM

FIREPLACE

SHELVES

DINING ROOM

VIEW ONTO THE GARDEN

29

# upwind
## house

STONES
FROM ABIQUIU

UNITED STATES
OF AMERICA

ABIQUIU

This house has been built in the USA, in the state of New Mexico, in a **windswept desert.** Because it stands on top of a **mesa** (a massive mountain that is flat as a pancake on top), it has to withstand both **turbulent winds** and **high temperatures.** You think living in such a place doesn't sound like fun? You might have a point there. But the house has been designed by Steven Holl, and that makes a difference.

IN ABIQUIU, SUMMERS
ARE SCORCHING HOT

COYOTE

ROADRUNNER
(STATE BIRD OF NEW MEXICO)

RABBITS

31

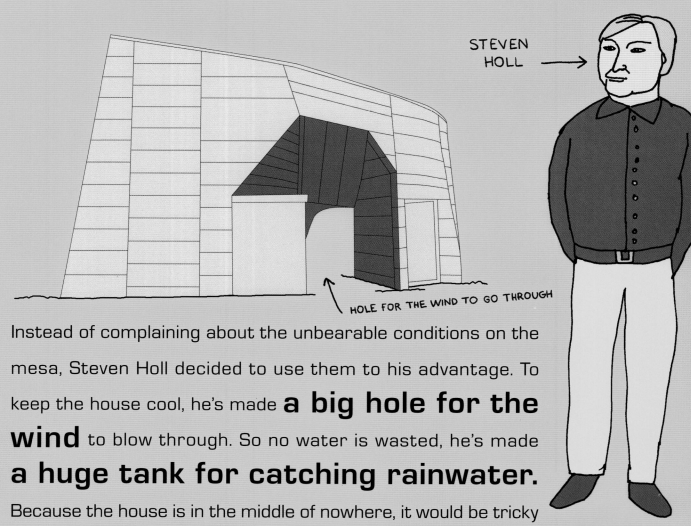

STEVEN HOLL

HOLE FOR THE WIND TO GO THROUGH

Instead of complaining about the unbearable conditions on the mesa, Steven Holl decided to use them to his advantage. To keep the house cool, he's made **a big hole for the wind** to blow through. So no water is wasted, he's made **a huge tank for catching rainwater.** Because the house is in the middle of nowhere, it would be tricky to lay electrical cables there. So the roof faces south and is covered with solar panels, which **convert sunlight into electricity.**

SOLAR PANEL

RAINWATER

HOLE FOR
THE WIND

The whole house is made of glimmering **aluminum,** which reflects heat. All the interior walls are **white.** ⇢ 

Bright colors reflect light and heat; dark colors absorb them. That's why white walls are cooler than dark walls.

The mesa is also home to various animals, so non-toxic materials have been used to construct this house.

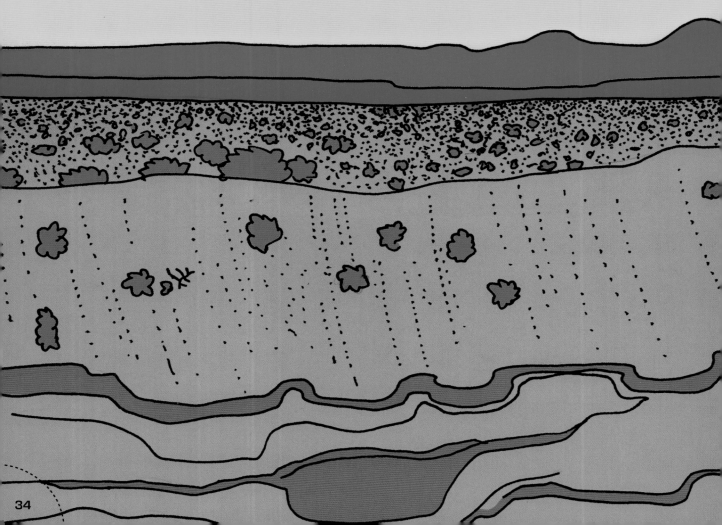

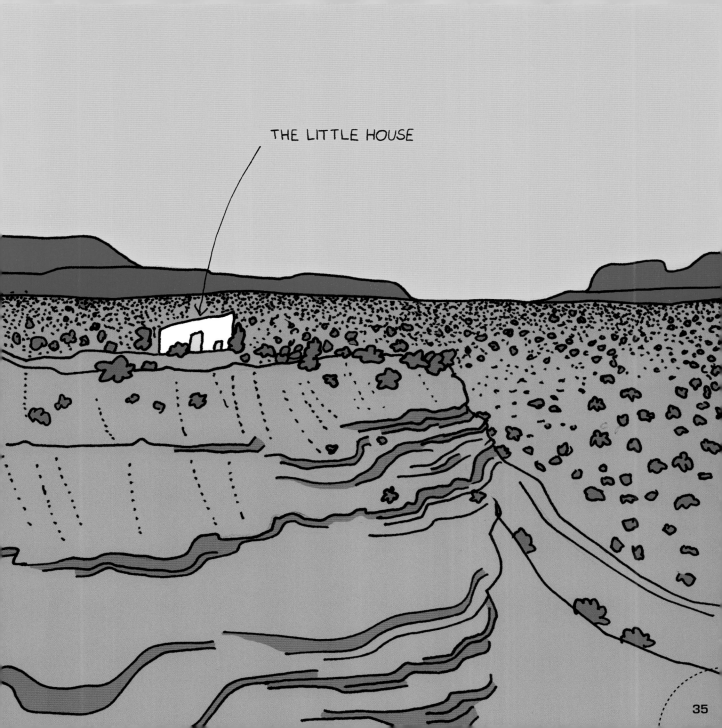

THE LITTLE HOUSE

35

▶ Tea House

# inflatable
## house

FRANKFURT
AM MAIN

GERMANY

Can you imagine **letting the air out of your house,** packing it into your suitcase, **then inflating it somewhere else?** Impossible? You're right—houses are huge and heavy. They have foundations. They have lots of solid and unwieldy elements, such as walls, floors and ceilings.

And yet the house built by Kengo Kuma in Frankfurt am Main, Germany, can be inflated and put up wherever you wish.

Granted, it's not an ordinary house where you can cook your dinner, watch TV or go to sleep. It is a specially-designed **house for drinking tea.** It has an electric stove for boiling water in a kettle. It also has nine tatami mats.

Traditional Japanese floor mat.

# curtain
## house

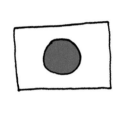

JAPAN

TOKYO

SHIGERU BAN

In Tokyo, the capital of Japan, there is a strange house with **enormous white curtains instead of walls.** It is the home of Mr and Mrs Takeshi and their two children. Mr Takeshi is a photographer. He grew up in a small, cramped house, which he didn't like, so as an adult he decided he'd had enough of living like that. He asked the architect Shigeru Ban to design him a spacious house.

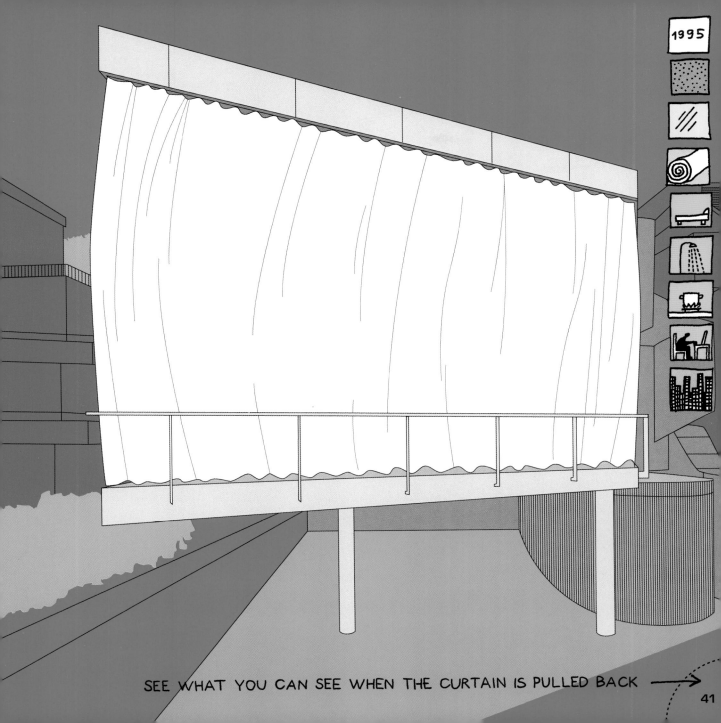

SEE WHAT YOU CAN SEE WHEN THE CURTAIN IS PULLED BACK ⟶

41

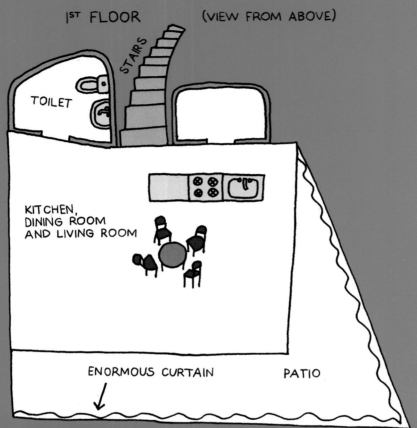

STAIRS

TOILET

KITCHEN,
DINING ROOM
AND LIVING ROOM

ENORMOUS CURTAIN        PATIO

Shigeru had a difficult puzzle to solve: how to construct a house that is cosy and private but, at the same time, **open to the outdoors?** He could have installed glass walls and hung curtains across them. But glass walls are too much like concrete walls—they shut a house off . . . Finally, he came up with a brilliant solution. No glass walls—just curtains!

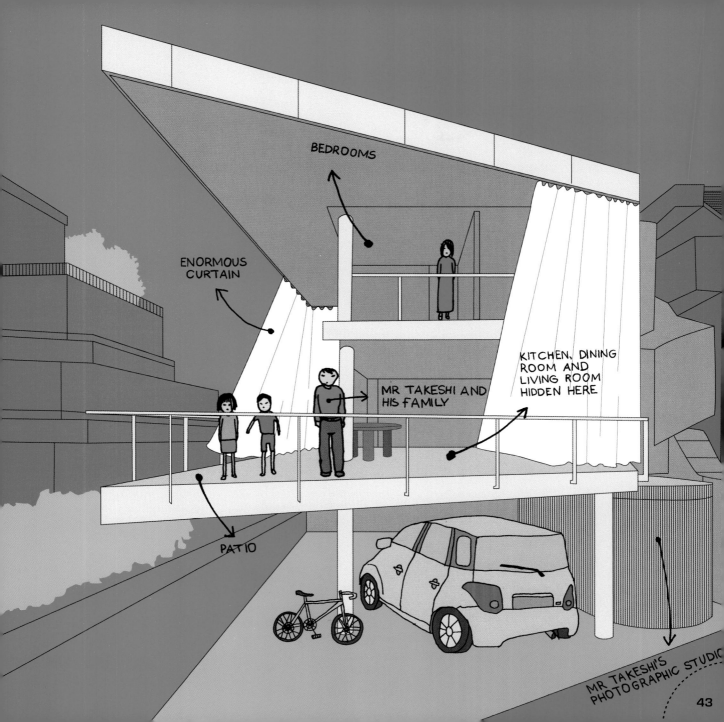

BEDROOMS

ENORMOUS
CURTAIN

KITCHEN, DINING
ROOM AND
LIVING ROOM
HIDDEN HERE

MR TAKESHI AND
HIS FAMILY

PATIO

MR TAKESHI'S
PHOTOGRAPHIC STUDIO

43

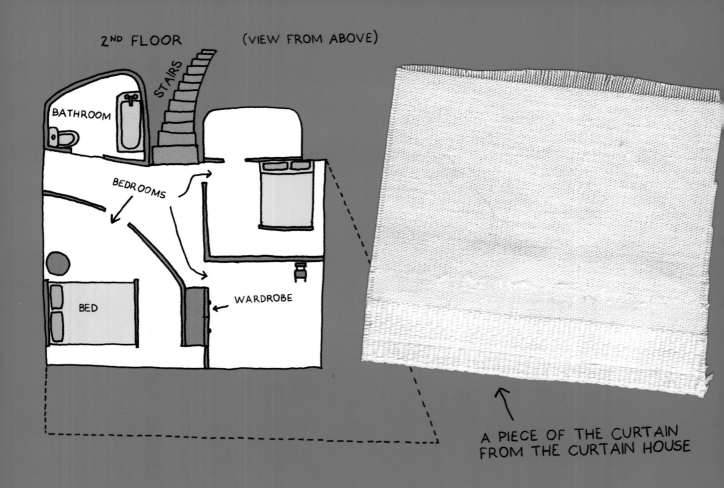

2ND FLOOR (VIEW FROM ABOVE)

STAIRS

BATHROOM

BEDROOMS

BED

WARDROBE

A PIECE OF THE CURTAIN
FROM THE CURTAIN HOUSE

Now Mr Takeshi's family can pull back the curtain and see what's happening in the street while they eat their dinner. They can also **pull the white curtain** and rest in one of the rooms, flooded with soft light.

BEDROOMS ON
THE TOP FLOOR

INDOORS WITH
THE CURTAIN DRAWN

KITCHEN, DINING ROOM
AND LIVING ROOM

45

# sand
## house

A hundred people turn to you for help. They have nowhere to live. They ask for **safe and comfortable houses, within a week.** Are you up to the challenge?

↑
NADER
KHALILI

Don't say, "Impossible! I'd need loads and loads of money. It takes more than a week to build one house, not to mention a hundred! And how would I build a house anyway?"

Instead, try out this thought: if you have no money, you could use materials that don't cost anything. If you don't have time or the necessary skills, think of something **simple to construct.**

IRAN

Follow Nader Khalili's example—he built a house out of long plastic bags filled with sand or soil.

BUILD YOUR OWN SAND HOUSE

MOULDS FOR FORMING DOORS AND WINDOWS

SANDBAGS PLACED IN CURVES

ENTRANCE

BEDROOM

MAIN ROOM

KITCHEN

HOUSE PLAN

TOOL FOR TAMPING DOWN THE SAND

# huge house with big spikes

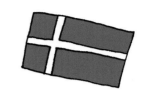

DENMARK

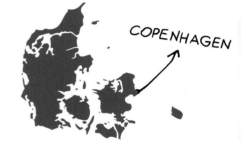

COPENHAGEN

When you see a **hedgehog** in the forest, or a **stout cactus** all covered with spikes, do you want to touch them? Do you want to check how prickly they feel, but you're a bit scared? Or do you just stand there, not sure, staring at the sharp tips of the thin needles . . .

This same spine-tingling sensation inspired the architects who designed a house with **spiky, pointed balconies.**

JULIEN DE SMEDT

BJARKE
INGELS

2005

51

AT THE BACK, THE HOUSE
HAS NO SPIKES. YOU CAN SEE
APARTMENTS THROUGH THE HUGE
PANELS OF GLASS.

BALCONY

NOBODY'S HOME,
SO IT'S DARK

┄┄┄┄► Free Spirit Sphere

# nut
## house

CANADA

VANCOUVER
ISLAND

Have you read stories about elves and other small forest creatures who inhabit a hollow in an old oak, a mushroom with a spotted hat or an acorn? Tom Chudleigh has always wanted to **feel like a forest elf.** That's why his house looks like a nut. A hazelnut, to be precise.

TOM CHUDLEIGH

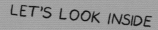

LET'S LOOK INSIDE ⟶

This **wooden ball,** or sphere, hangs from a web of ropes. Inside the sphere there is a bed, a table, cupboards and other things to make you comfortable. When you sleep in this nut, you become **part of the forest.** That's what's so brilliant about it. You aren't an intruder, but a forest dweller. You cause **no damage to the environment.** The hanging house is ecological; it is made of wood, which is a renewable material. It doesn't ooze any toxic substances. And it doesn't need any foundations!

WILLEM
EUTELINGS

MICHIEL
RIEDIJK

2003

61

CAN YOU SPOT THE LIKENESS BETWEEN

# MEET THE UFO RESIDENTS

# caterpillar
## house

JAPAN

YAIZU

DOOR

A Japanese man, who loved making clay pots, saved up enough money for a new Toyota. But on his way to the car dealer, he suddenly changed his mind. He decided to spend the money on **a ceramics studio** instead, where he could also show off his pots. So he asked the Mount Fuji Architects to build him one **for the price of the car.**

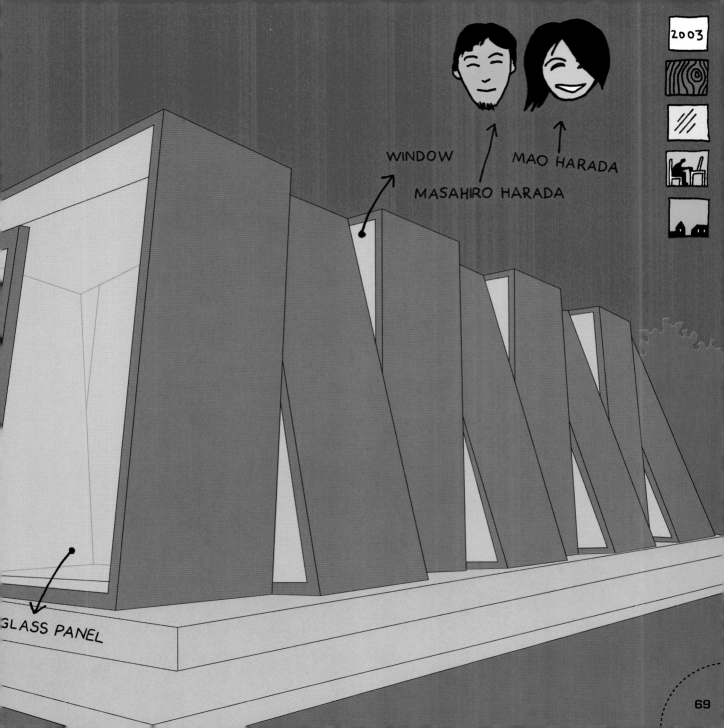

WINDOW

MASAHIRO HARADA

MAO HARADA

2003

GLASS PANEL

69

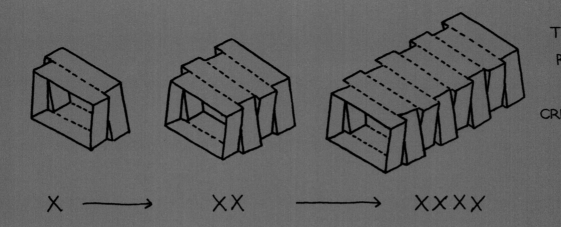

X $\longrightarrow$  XX  $\longrightarrow$  XXXX

TWO LEANING
RECTANGLES
MAKE ONE
CRISS-CROSSED X

# Masahiro and Mao Harada liked the

challenge—an automobile competing with architecture!

They didn't mind that their client had only a small amount of money, because they had a great idea. The Mount Fuji Architects thought up a house made out of **four Xs.** Each X was assembled out of two rectangles put together at an angle.

Because of its shape, the studio was called **XXXX House.** All the gaps were filled with glass panes to make it warm. And then, very gently, this wooden caterpillar was placed in its garden.

WHAT ELSE
COULD OLD
WATER
TOWERS BE
USED FOR?

# igloo
## house

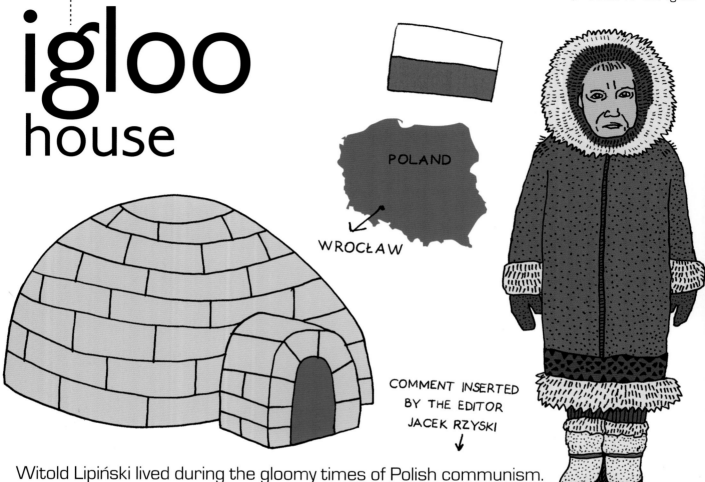

POLAND

WROCŁAW

COMMENT INSERTED
BY THE EDITOR
JACEK RZYSKI
↓

WITOLD LIPIŃSKI
IN TRADITIONAL
INUIT CLOTHES

Witold Lipiński lived during the gloomy times of Polish communism.

He couldn't even dream of travelling to South Berlin, let alone

something more extravagant, like a trip to the Moon—not even a

visit to **Greenland,** where Inuit people live in their igloos.

So he built himself **a little igloo** on his small plot of land.

1963

81

# suitcase house

CHINA

BADALING

ARCHITECT
GARY CHANG

Have you ever wondered how much space is wasted in each room of your house? Take the bathroom, for instance. How long do you spend there each day? Less than one hour? Maybe two? (Some people spend hours in there!)

**Wouldn't it be less wasteful, if rooms appeared only when needed?** That's exactly what happens inside a strangely flexible house built in China, not far from the Great Wall.

The **space** inside this suitcase house can be **divided any way you wish,** thanks to special walls—partitions—that can be moved. Extra rooms are hidden under the floor: a kitchen, bedrooms, a storage room, library, music room, study. There's even a sauna!

# blue houses
# on the roof

THE NETHERLANDS

ROTTERDAM

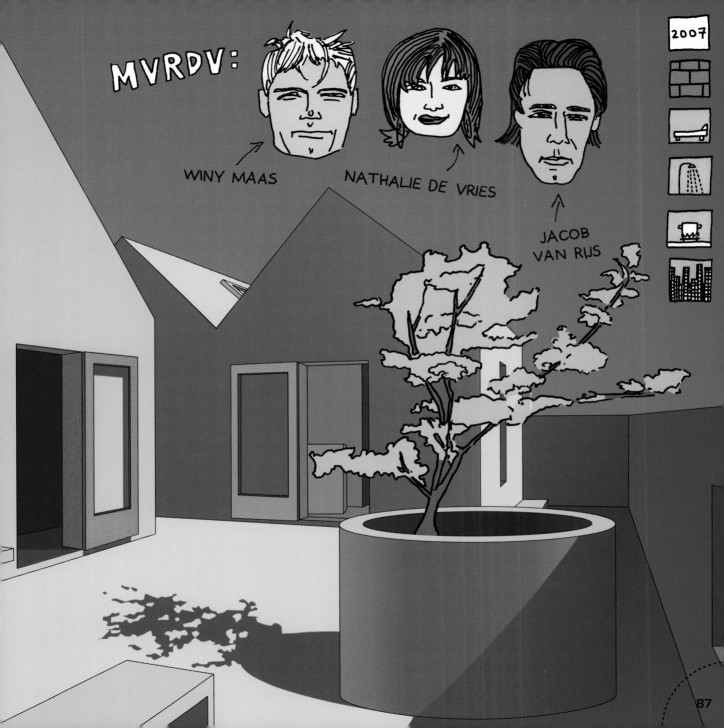

If you climbed up to the roof of a house in a big town, you might not be impressed by the colors. Brown and grey are everywhere, and there's not much of a view—more like a dirty stain.

The Dutch MVRDV architects wanted to **change the grim panorama** of their native Rotterdam.

BEAUTY IN THE WINDOW

SECRET ADMIRER

THE NEIGHBOUR'S UGLY WIFE

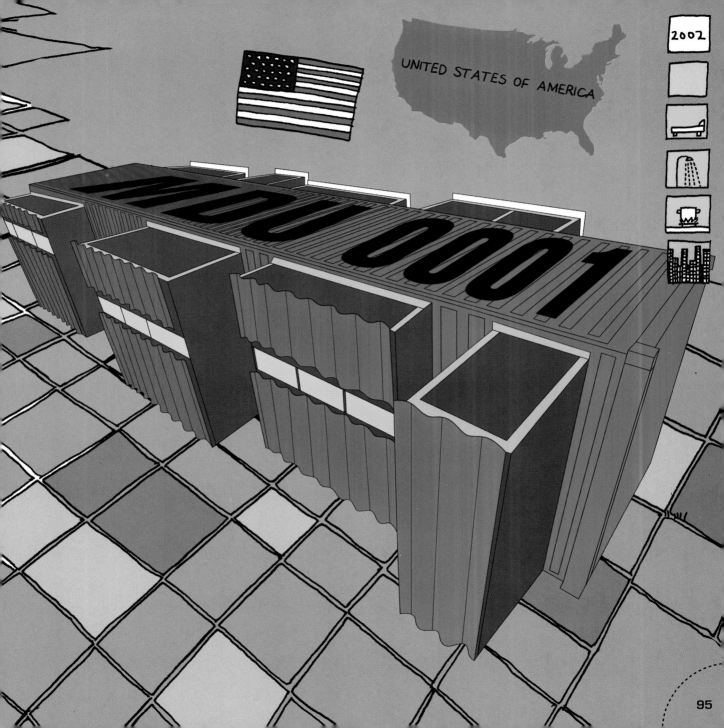

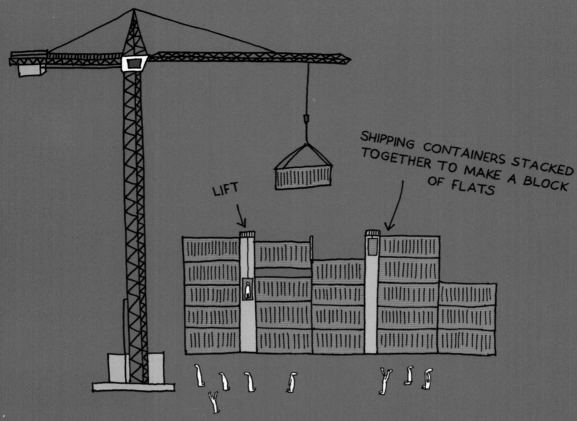

LIFT

SHIPPING CONTAINERS STACKED TOGETHER TO MAKE A BLOCK OF FLATS

Giuseppe Lignano and Ada Tolla liked the idea of a **house inside a big box** that can **travel anywhere in the world.** But they had an even better idea: instead of one box, how about a whole bunch? **Stacked one upon another,** they create ready-made **apartment blocks.**

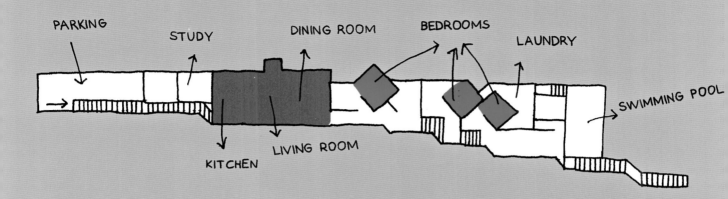

VIEW FROM ABOVE

PARKING
STUDY
DINING ROOM
BEDROOMS
LAUNDRY
SWIMMING POOL
KITCHEN
LIVING ROOM

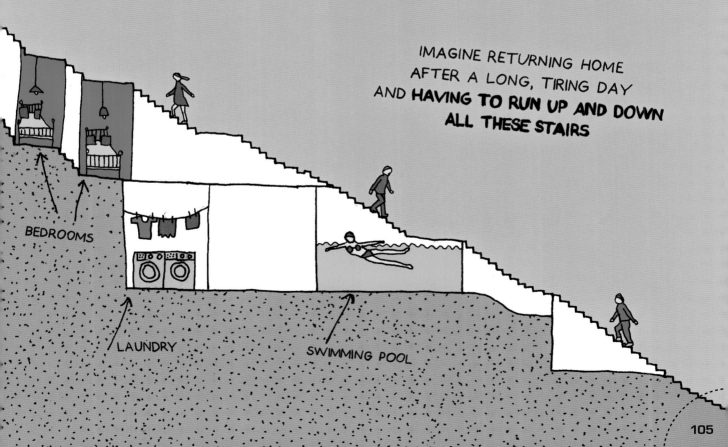

IMAGINE RETURNING HOME
AFTER A LONG, TIRING DAY
AND **HAVING TO RUN UP AND DOWN
ALL THESE STAIRS**

BEDROOMS

LAUNDRY
SWIMMING POOL

# house of building
# blocks

MICHAEL
JANTZEN

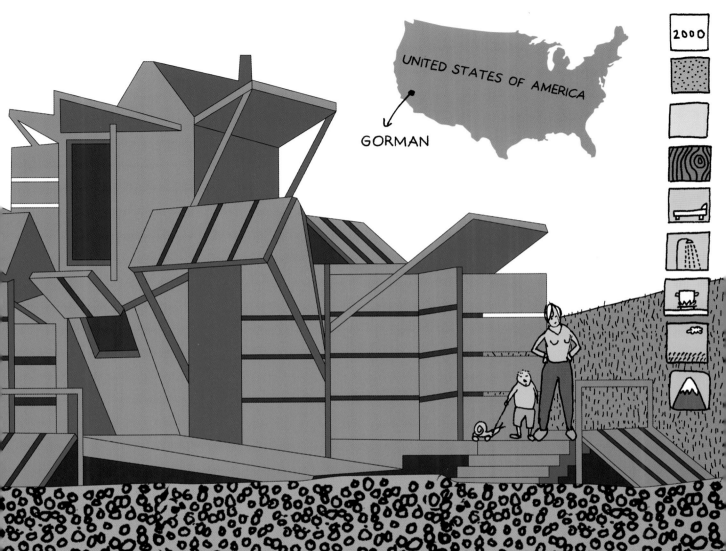

UNITED STATES OF AMERICA

GORMAN

2000

107

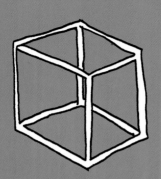
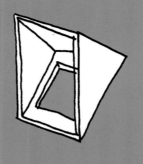

Are you sometimes bored with how your room looks? The same old four walls? If only you could **move all the walls**—wouldn't that be great! And make some new windows. Or add an extra door . . .

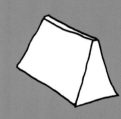

Michael Jantzen often gets bored with houses. So he thought of a building which can be easily transformed. It's easy. **Take it apart** and **put it back together,** any way you like.

First, you construct cube frames out of special pipes. Then you interlock the cubes into the shape of your dream house.

You can attach different panels, partitions, walls, doors and so on. All the parts fold into or out of the cubes, so you're **free to experiment.** Because all the parts match perfectly, you could even swap with your neighbor!

2003

117

CHIMNEY

WINTER

IN SUMMER THE HOUSE STICKS ITS HEAD OUT

**In winter the house shrinks**—that's how it keeps warm. In summer it extends as far as it can to let in more sun and to look across the lake.

The part that sticks out is covered inside with **reindeer skins,** traditionally used in northern Scandinavia for insulation during cold winters. The house has no electricity, no running water and no heating. It's got a stove, though!

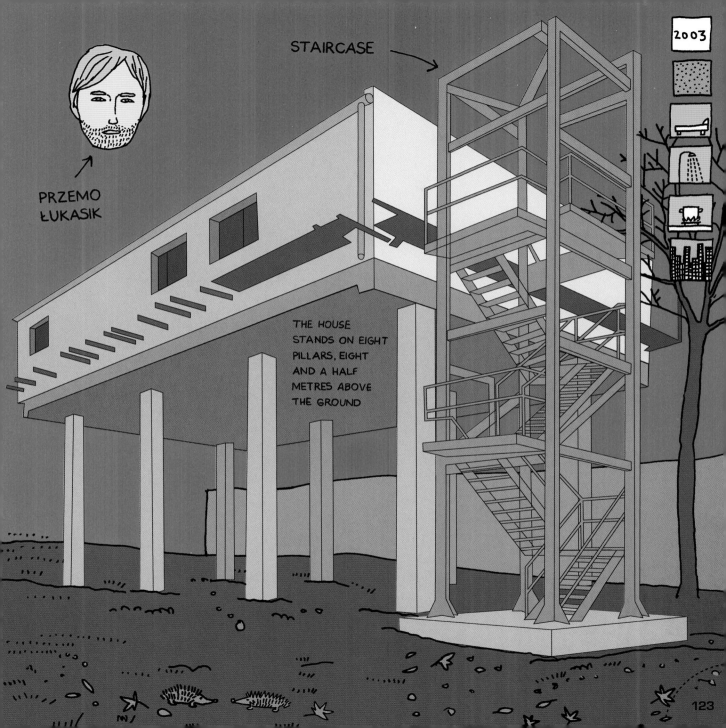

STAIRCASE

PRZEMO ŁUKASIK

THE HOUSE
STANDS ON EIGHT
PILLARS, EIGHT
AND A HALF
METRES ABOVE
THE GROUND

2003

123

OLD MINING LAMPS

A NEW LAMP

Many years passed. One day Przemyslaw Łukasik, nicknamed Przemo, arrived in Bytom. He bought the ground above White Eagle together with all its buildings.

The people of Bytom were worried. Would Przemo demolish the **old lamp house**—the building where the superhuman miners had kept their precious lamps?

To their relief, the lamp house survived. Przemo didn't bring destruction. Instead he brought reconstruction. He converted the lamp house into a spacious loft that proudly exhibits the heroic mining past of Bytom.

# butterfly
## house

LAURIE CHETWOOD

SURREY

GREAT BRITAIN

In nature, change doesn't happen suddenly. Everything evolves gradually. Take, for instance, the butterfly. First, there's an **egg.** Out of the egg comes a **caterpillar,** which transforms into a **chrysalis.** Out of the chrysalis emerges a **butterfly,** which lives for a couple of hours or a couple of days. The butterfly lays **new eggs.** And the whole cycle repeats.

Butterfly House captures this **life cycle.** The organic form of the house—its glass panels, tangled wires and bungee ropes, netted fiber-optic cables, bright sails—resembles a living body that changes with the passage of time.

2003

127

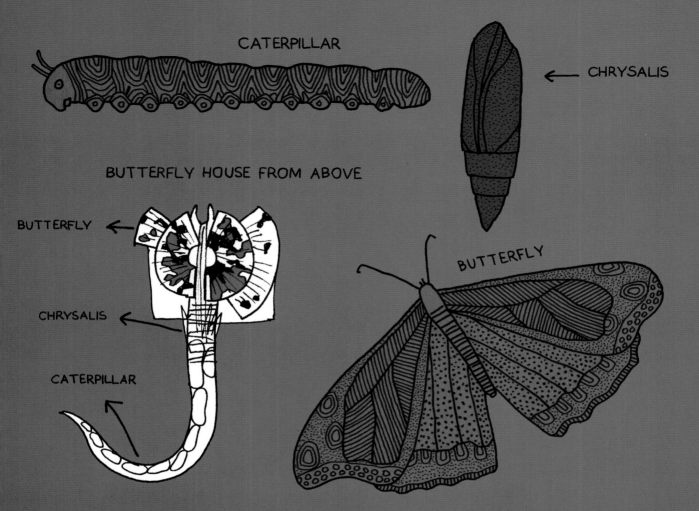

CATERPILLAR

CHRYSALIS

BUTTERFLY HOUSE FROM ABOVE

BUTTERFLY

CHRYSALIS

CATERPILLAR

BUTTERFLY

**The garden imitates the early stages in the life of the butterfly.** The building itself shows the moment when the butterfly finally leaves its cocoon and unfurls its wings for the first time.

THE HOUSE
IS FULL
OF WEIRD
FURNITURE

HANGING
ARMCHAIRS

129

# sail
## house

Casa de Retiro Espiritual

SPAIN

NOT FAR
FROM SEVILLE

EMILIO
AMBASZ

Imagine a house that has only **two tall white walls** that look like sails—a house that has all its rooms under the ground, with just **a patio and a fountain** between the rooms and the sails. From the patio, narrow metal stairs lead up to a carved wooden balcony, which looks like a traditional **Andalusian watchtower.**

> That's an inner courtyard

> Andalusia is a region in southern Spain

And now imagine that a particular architect from Argentina, Emilio Ambasz, has constructed this fantasy house. Architecture, just like the imagination, has no borders.

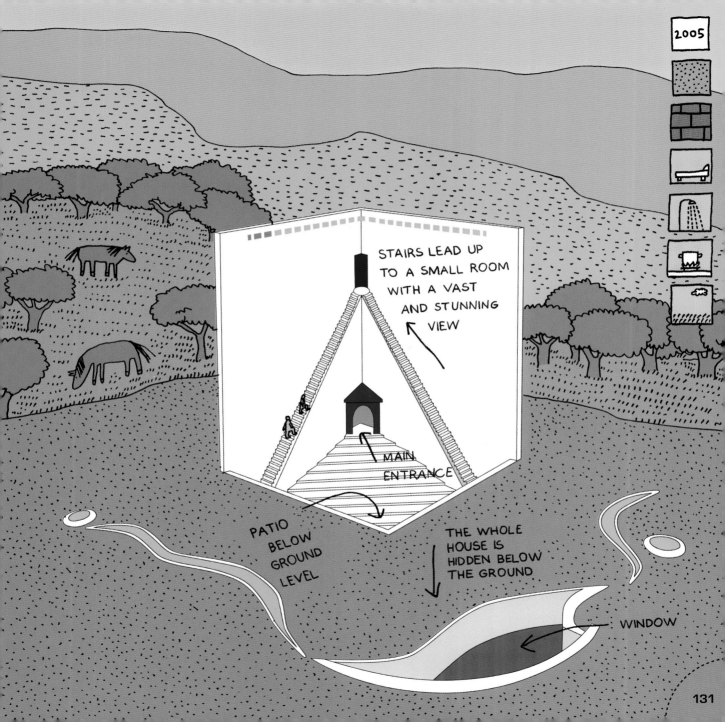

2005

STAIRS LEAD UP
TO A SMALL ROOM
WITH A VAST
AND STUNNING
VIEW

MAIN
ENTRANCE

PATIO
BELOW
GROUND
LEVEL

THE WHOLE
HOUSE IS
HIDDEN BELOW
THE GROUND

WINDOW

131

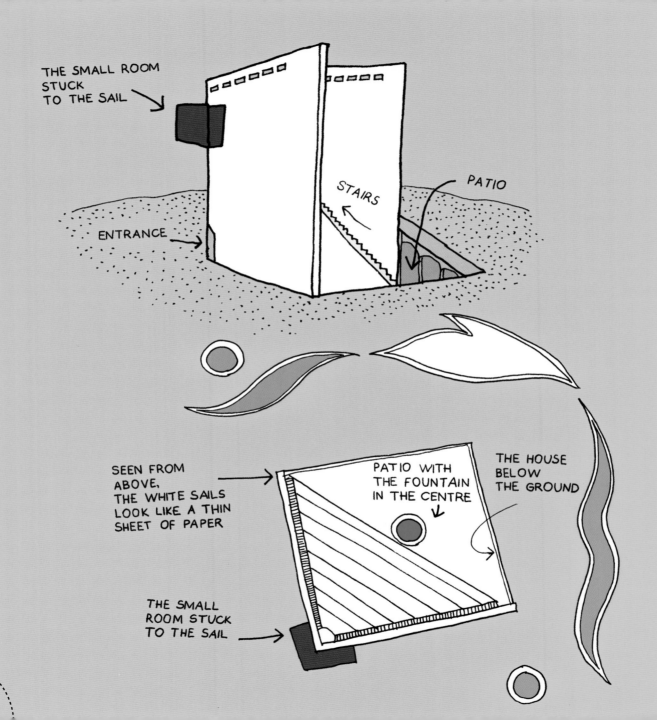

THE SMALL ROOM
STUCK
TO THE SAIL

STAIRS

PATIO

ENTRANCE

SEEN FROM
ABOVE,
THE WHITE SAILS
LOOK LIKE A THIN
SHEET OF PAPER

PATIO WITH
THE FOUNTAIN
IN THE CENTRE

THE HOUSE
BELOW
THE GROUND

THE SMALL
ROOM STUCK
TO THE SAIL

PATIO

133

# see-through house

WERNER SOBEK

Do you hate it when **someone uninvited turns up in your room, and looks it up and down?** That crazy aunt, back from overseas. The busy-body neighbor who lives in the house opposite. To protect your privacy, you draw all the curtains and hang the No Entry!!! sign on your door.

But there are people who don't mind being open to view. They don't treat their house as a hideaway or a bunker—instead they **embrace the uninvited gaze.** Their houses have no curtains; some don't even have concrete walls. For example, Werner Sobek's house is completely and utterly see-through.

GERMANY

STUTTGART

2000

135

Only a **huge glass panel** separates all the rooms (except for the toilet) from the garden. **Even the bathtub can be seen from outside!** Now everyone can watch Werner Sobek enjoying his bath.

# pipe
## house

Das Parkhotel

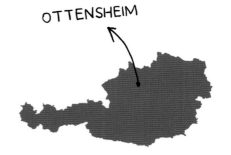

OTTENSHEIM

AUSTRIA

How about **living in the sewers?** You must be joking! But what if we take a pipe—a new giant concrete sewage pipe—and cut it, and drill a small hole for a window, and add a wall at the back and a door at the front . . . then put a double bed inside? **The house is ready!**

And that's exactly what Andreas Strauss has done. Actually, he's made a whole hotel out of pipes. Now everyone can spend a night in a sewage pipe. Don't think: filthy rats and cockroaches! **Think: an elegant, habitable pipe** equipped with a lamp, a light cotton sleeping bag and a woolly blanket.

ANDREAS
STRAUSS
SLEEPING

2005

139

Treetent

# pear
## house

THE NETHERLANDS

DRÉ WAPENAAR

You might have heard of **tree lovers**—people who tie themselves to trees, so it's impossible to cut these trees down; people who live in the trees to protect them.

Especially for tree lovers, Dré Wapenaar has invented a house shaped like a pear. He figured it's much nicer and warmer to **sleep inside a house tied to the tree trunk** than to be tied to the tree trunk with a metal chain on a cold night.

143

# 4×4
## house

TADAO
ANDO

JAPAN

KOBE

DESTROYER

VARAN
THE FLYING LIZARD

MECHAGODZILLA

RODAN
THE BIRD OF DEATH

MOTHRA
THE GIANT MOTH

GAMERA
THE GIANT
FLYING TURTLE

TWO LITTLE MOTHRAS
SOON THEY'LL GROW
THEIR WINGS

GODZILLA  NUCLEAR
BREATH

MONSTER ZERO
THE THREE-HEADED
DRAGON

MONSTERS
THAT KEEP
ATTACKING JAPAN

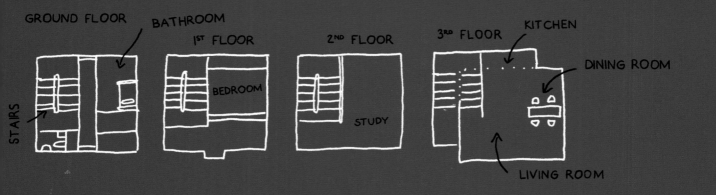

GROUND FLOOR
BATHROOM
1ST FLOOR
2ND FLOOR
3RD FLOOR
KITCHEN
DINING ROOM
STAIRS
BEDROOM
STUDY
LIVING ROOM

**4×4.** It's nothing to do with off-road vehicles, but **it is all about the number 4.**

Tadao Ando can't resist the number **4**. He has built a seafront house which has **4** levels. Each level is a square, **4** meters wide by **4** meters long. The square itself is the perfect geometric shape for the number **4** (it has **4** equal sides and **4** equal angles). The top floor of the house is a cube **4** meters high, **4** meters deep and **4** meters wide. And if you want some more number **4**, think about each of the six walls of the cube—all **4** by **4**.

By now you should have no doubts—the name **4×4** is **4** times better than any other name Tadao Ando might have chosen for his house.

THERE ARE FREQUENT EARTHQUAKES IN JAPAN. THIS MEANS THAT ELECTRICAL CABLES AREN'T ALLOWED TO RUN UNDER BUILDINGS OR ROADS, AND BIG JAPANESE CITIES LOOK LIKE GIGANTIC COBWEBS.

Maison à Bordeaux

# lift
## house

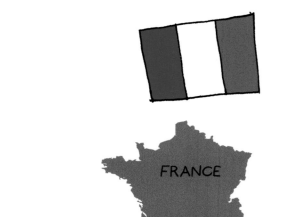

FRANCE

BORDEAUX

There was a man in France who couldn't walk. He had to use a wheelchair. Trying to get around a small house in a wheelchair can be very difficult and frustrating.

So he asked Rem Koolhaas to design a **special house for a person in a wheelchair.** He knew that the new house would structure his daily life, so he wanted a truly imaginative solution.

REM KOOLHAAS

1998

149

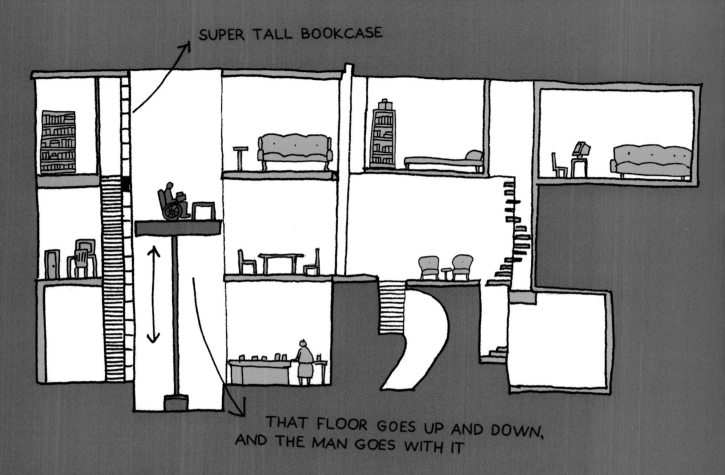

SUPER TALL BOOKCASE

THAT FLOOR GOES UP AND DOWN,
AND THE MAN GOES WITH IT

And he's got it!

The house has three levels, each with a specific function. All the levels are connected by a huge platform that moves up and down like **a lift that's as big as a room.** When the lift stops at one of the levels, it becomes part of the floor.

Casa Poli

# house at the edge
# of the world

CHILE

COLIUMO

To live at the edge of the world, **almost falling off the map,** with only rocks and ocean to keep you company . . . That's what Mauricio Pezo and Sofia von Ellrichshausen dreamt about. So they built a house on top of a steep cliff, battered by crashing waves.

In the olden days, people didn't know that the earth is round. They thought they lived on a giant flat plate with a huge waterfall at its edge. Standing by the ocean, they thought the horizon was **the edge of the world.**

That's how the residents of this house feel when they wake up and look out onto the vast expanse of the sea.

LOTS OF PELICANS LIVE NEARBY →

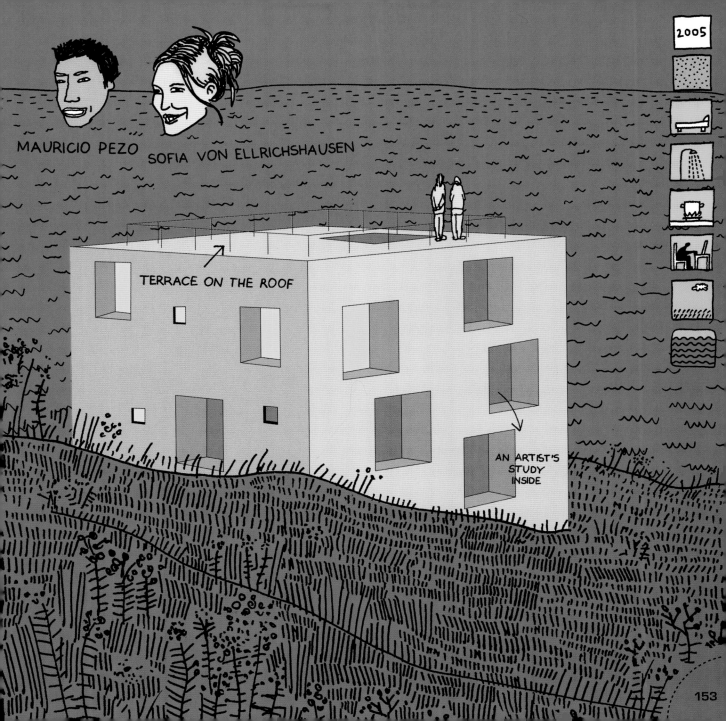

JELLYFISH

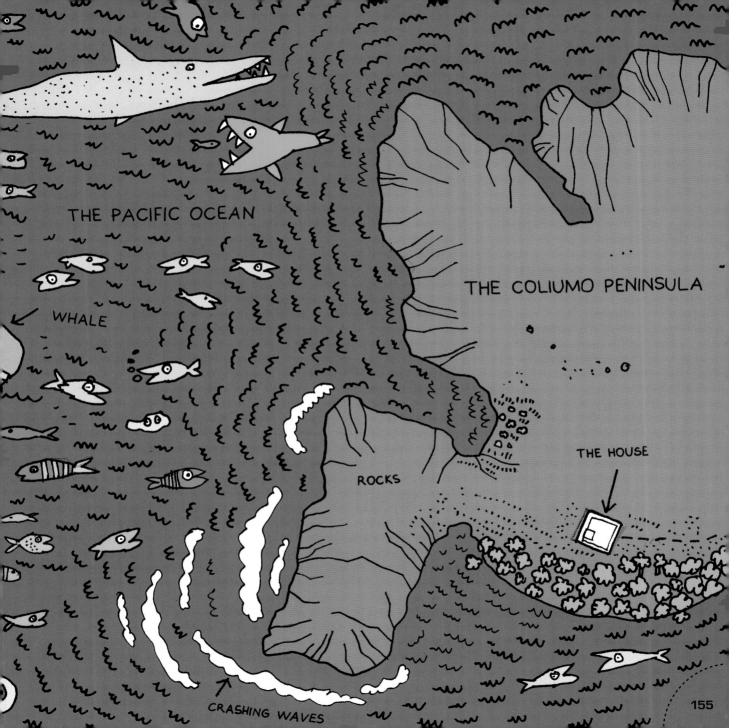

THE PACIFIC OCEAN

WHALE

THE COLIUMO PENINSULA

THE HOUSE

ROCKS

CRASHING WAVES

155

# Index

**H.O.U.S.E.**

HarperCollins books may be purchased for educational, business, or sales promotional use. For information please write: Special Markets Department, HarperCollins Publishers, 10 East 53rd Street, New York, NY 10022.

Published in 2012 by
Harper Design
An Imprint of HarperCollins Publishers
10 East 53rd Street
New York, NY 10022
Tel: (212) 207-7000
Fax: (212) 207-7654
harperdesign@harpercollins.com
www.harpercollins.com

Distributed throughout the world by
HarperCollins Publishers
10 East 53rd Street
New York, NY 10022
Fax: (212) 207-7654

Library of Congress Control Number: 2011943838
ISBN 978-0-06-211375-7

Printed in China
First Printing, 2012